Family Life 2

STUDENT EDITION

David Thomas, PhD

General Editor

RCL Benziger®

Allen, Texas

The Subcommittee on the Catechism, United States Conference of Catholic Bishops, has found this text, copyright 2011, to be in conformity with the *Catechism of the Catholic Church*; it may be used only as supplemental to other basal catechetical texts.

Consultants

Paul Duckro, PhD
Tim Hogan, PsyD
Tom Everson
Fanny Pedraza

NIHIL OBSTAT
Rev. Msgr. Robert Coerver
Censor Librorum

IMPRIMATUR
† Most Reverend Kevin J. Farrell DD
Bishop of Dallas

May 3, 2010

The *Nihil Obstat* and *Imprimatur* are official declarations that the material reviewed is free of doctrinal or moral error. No implication is contained therein that those granting the *Nihil Obstat* and *Imprimatur* agree with the contents, opinions, or statements expressed.

Send all inquiries to:
RCL Benziger
206 East Bethany Drive
Allen, TX 75002-3804

Toll Free   877-275-4725
Fax   800-688-8356

Visit us at www.RCLBenziger.com/FamilyLife

20652   ISBN 978-0-7829-1502-0 (Student Edition)
20662   ISBN 978-0-7829-1512-9 (Parent Connection)
20682   ISBN 978-0-7829-1532-7 (Teacher Edition)

3rd printing.
Manufactured for RCL Benziger in Cincinnati, OH, USA.
July 2011.

RCL Benziger Development Team

James Spurgin
Editor

Tricia Legault
Design

Laura Fremder
Production

Daniel S. Mulhall
National Catechetical Advisor

Jo Rotunno
Director of Catechist and Professional Development

Susan Smith
Director of Project Development

Ed DeStefano
Publisher

Peter M. Esposito
President

ACKNOWLEDGMENTS

Excerpts from the *New American Bible* with Revised New Testament and Revised Psalms © 1991, 1986, 1970 Confraternity of Christian Doctrine, Washington, D.C. and are used by permission of the copyright owner. All Rights Reserved. No part of the New American Bible may be reproduced in any form without permission in writing from the copyright owner.

PHOTO CREDITS

Cover, Alloy Photography/Veer; Page 3; Ariel Skelley/Corbis; 4, SW Productions/Gettyimages; 5, Ariel Skelley/Corbis; 7, Jose Luis Pelaez Inc/Gettyimages; 8, David Young-Wolf/Photoedit; 11, Lori Adamski Peek/Gettyimages; 13, SuperStock/Gettyimages; 14, Stockbroker/SuperStock; 16, Myrleen Ferguson Cate/Photoedi; 21, Scout J Photography/Gettyimages; 25, iStock; 29, Brand X Pictures/Gettyimages; 30, Jose Luis Pelaez Inc/Gettyimages; 31, Tetra Images/Gettyimages; 32, Asia Images/Gettyimages; 34, Altrendo Images/Gettyimages; 39, Pixland/Punchstock; 41, Gettyimages; 42, Myrleen Ferguson Cate/Photoedit; 45, Blend Images/Veer; 46, George Doyle/Gettyimages; 46, Valuline/Punchstock; 49, Flying Colours Ltd/Gettyimages; 52, Jupiterimages/Gettyimages; 54, Philippe Lissac/Corbis; 55, iStock

CONTENTS

The Catholic Home

Your Life with Jesus

When you were baptized, you became a child of God.
God gave you the gifts of faith, hope and love.
You can talk to God in prayer.
You can choose to do what is right and good.
When you choose to do right, you are following Jesus.
This is how you can follow Jesus:

1. Attend Mass with your family on Sundays and on Holy Days of Obligation.

2. Read and talk about the Bible with your family.

3. Pray every day.

4. Be kind to others.

5. Help your family.

Family Prayer

Heavenly Father, you have given us
the Holy Family of Jesus, Mary and Joseph
as a beautiful model for our family.
Help us to be open to your Spirit,
so we may always do what is good and right.
Help us to care for each other
and to do your will.
Amen.

Prayers to Learn

Sign of the Cross

In the name of the Father,
and of the Son,
and of the Holy Spirit.
Amen.

The Lord's Prayer

Our Father,
  who art in heaven,
  hallowed be thy name.
Thy kingdom come;
  thy will be done
  on earth as it is in heaven.
Give us this day our daily bread,
  and forgive us our trespasses
  as we forgive those who
  trespass against us.
And lead us not into temptation,
  but deliver us from evil.
Amen.

Glory Prayer

Glory be to the Father,
and to the Son,
and to the Holy Spirit:
as it was in the beginning,
is now and ever shall be,
world without end. Amen.

Hail Mary

Hail Mary, full of grace,
  the Lord is with thee.
Blessed art thou among women,
  and blessed is the fruit
  of thy womb, Jesus.
Holy Mary, Mother of God,
  pray for us sinners,
  now, and at the hour
  of our death.
Amen.

Prayer to My Guardian Angel

Angel of God, my guardian dear,
to whom God's love commits me here.
Ever this day be at my side
to light, to guard, to rule and guide.
Amen.

Morning Prayer

Dear God,
as I begin this day,
keep me in your love and care.
Help me to live as your child today.
Bless me, my family and my friends.
Keep us all close to you.
Amen.

Evening Prayer

Dear God,
I thank you for today.
Keep me safe throughout the night.
Bless those who love and care for me.
I love you and know you love me too.
Amen.

Grace before Meals

Bless us, O Lord,
and these thy gifts,
which we are
about to receive
from thy bounty,
through Christ Our Lord.
Amen.

Grace after Meals

We give you thanks
for these and all your gifts,
Almighty God.
You live and rule forever.
Amen.

A Vocation Prayer

God, I know you will call me
for special work in my life.
Help me to follow Jesus each day
and be ready to answer your call.
Amen.

Family Living

The Great Commandment

"You shall love the Lord, your God, with all your heart, with all your soul, and with all your mind. . . . You shall love your neighbor as yourself." (Matthew 22:37–39)

Jesus' Commandment

"This is my commandment: love one another as I love you."

(John 15:12)

The Ten Commandments

1. I am the Lord your God: you shall not have strange gods before me.
2. You shall not take the name of the Lord your God in vain.
3. Remember to keep holy the Lord's Day.
4. Honor your father and your mother.
5. You shall not kill.
6. You shall not commit adultery.
7. You shall not steal.
8. You shall not lie.
9. You shall not covet your neighbor's wife.
10. You shall not covet your neighbor's goods.

(based on Exodus 20:2–3, 7–17)

God with Us

Jesus was called "Emmanuel," which means "God is with us." Jesus said, "I will always be with you" *(based on Matthew 1:23, 28:20)*.

When our family is sad, Jesus is there to comfort us. When our family is happy, Jesus is there to share our happiness. In all aspects of our family life, God is with us.

Jerusalem, Jerusalem!
by James Tissot (1836–1902 French)

Healthy Habits in the Home

As a family, review the Ten Commandments as good rules for the family to live by. Take time to explain the reasons for all of your family rules. Make sure that everyone knows what the rules are and understands the reasons for them.

Family Blessings

Bless one another with the Sign of the Cross. Think about how this prayer reminds you that God the Father, God the Son and God the Holy Spirit are present with us every day.

Taking the Lesson Home

Ask your child to read this story to the family.

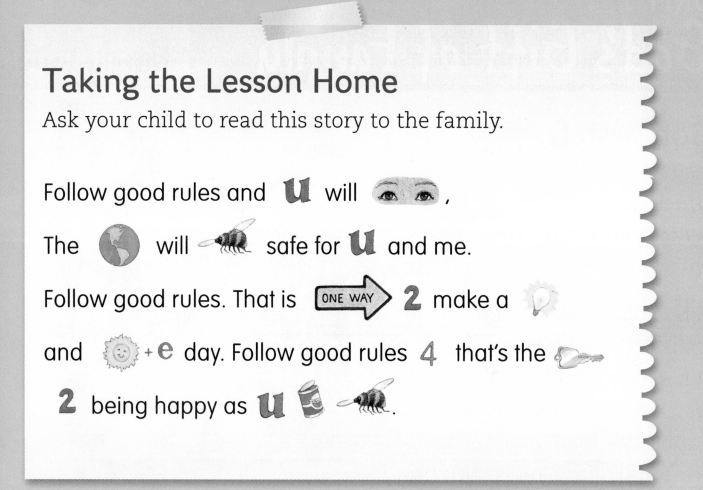

Follow good rules and **u** will [eyes],

The [globe] will [bee] safe for **u** and me.

Follow good rules. That is ONE WAY → **2** make a [lightbulb]

and [sun] + **e** day. Follow good rules **4** that's the [key]

2 being happy as **u** [can] [bee].

Faith on the Fridge

God is always
present with
our family.

Family
Web Time
RCLBFamilyLife.com

LESSON
1

God Made Families

God created all kinds of people.
God made all kinds of families.
And God loves us all.

God wants members of a family
to love one another.
God wants members of a family
to share time together.
That is God's plan.

 How do people in your family show each other love?

God Loves Families

Catholics Believe
God loves
every family.

Think about the families you know.
Each one is a little different.
A family has a mother and a father.
A family may have one sister and
two brothers.

A family may have just one parent.
A child may live with grandparents
or other relatives.
A child might be adopted.
"Adopted" means that the child was
chosen to be part of a family forever.
Some children are part of more
than one family.
God loves all families.

Use the picture frame
below to draw a picture
of the people in your
family. Be sure to draw
yourself in the picture.

"Welcome, Jesus"

Jesus made a wonderful promise.
He said, "I am with you always."

(Matthew 28:20)

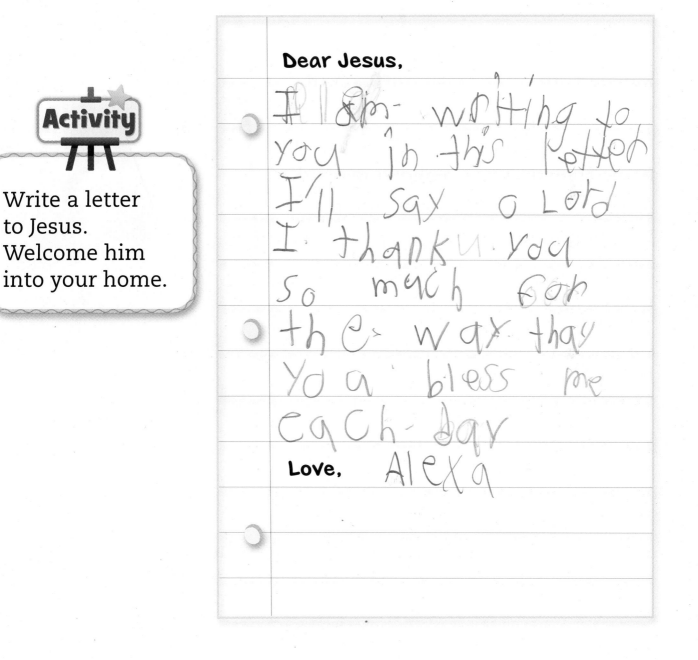

Activity

Write a letter to Jesus. Welcome him into your home.

Dear Jesus,

I am writing to you in this letter I'll say o Lord I thank you so much for the way that you a bless me each day

Love, Alexa

Rules and Choices

Why Rules?

All families have good rules. Good rules help us live as God wants us to live.

Maybe your family has rules about mealtimes and homework. Maybe your family has rules for watching TV and using the computer. Following good family rules can keep you safe and help you to be happy. Following good rules helps us live as Jesus taught us to live.

Jesus taught the most important rule: He said, "Love God with your whole heart, and love others as you love yourself" *(based on Matthew 22:37–39)*.

 How do good rules help you stay happy and well?

Do Your Best

I try hard to obey good family rules.
Sometimes I forget to follow the rules.
Sometimes I do not stop and think
about what might happen next.

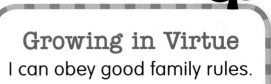

Growing in Virtue
I can obey good family rules.

When I break a rule, I can say,
"I am sorry" to God.
I can also say, "I am sorry"
to anyone I hurt.
I can then say to myself,
"I can do better."
I can do my best to obey good rules.

Read each sentence in the chart.
Color the box that shows how
often you do the action described.

ACTION	NEVER	SOMETIMES	ALWAYS
I ask, "Can I help you?"			
I follow directions.			
I pick up my things.			
I say, "I am sorry."			

I Obey God's Rules

The Ten Commandments
are God's rules.
They keep my family
and me happy and safe.
They keep everyone
happy and safe.

Here are some of God's rules:

- Love God.
- Honor and respect your parents.
- Keep Sunday a holy day.
- Don't hurt anybody.
- Tell the truth. Don't tell lies.
- Don't take things that aren't yours.

Choose one of God's rules.
Write what you will do to obey that rule.

I will _____

_____

_____.

Name _____

Summary

We have learned about God's Gift of Family.

LESSON 1: God's Plan

- God loves every family.
- There are many kinds of families.
- God is present with us in our family.

LESSON 2: Rules and Choices

- Good rules keep us healthy, holy and safe.
- Every good rule has a reason.
- I can obey good rules.

Content Review

Complete each sentence using one word from the word bank.

break	family	plan

1. God loves every ....

2. Families are part of God's ....

3. When I .... a rule, I can say, "I am sorry."

Circle the T if the sentence is true. Circle the F if the sentence is false.

1. God wants each member of a family to love one another.　　T　　F
2. God only loves some families.　　T　　F
3. Good family rules help families live as God wants us to live.　　T　　F
4. Jesus gave us rules to keep families happy and safe.　　T　　F
5. Some rules are not good rules and do not help families live as God wants them to live.　　T　　F

Name _____

Thinking It Through

**Read each question. Then write a short response.
Share your answers.**

1. What are some things families do together?

_____

_____

2. How can you show love to your family?

_____

_____

3. What can you do if you think a rule is not good?

_____

_____

Working Together

Think of good rules for your classroom.
Write them on a piece of paper.
Share your rules with the class.
Discuss how the rules are good.

Sharing Our Gifts

When Saint Thomas Aquinas went to school, people did not think he was very smart. They even called him a "dumb ox." He sat in his seat without talking, day after day. But he was listening carefully. That was one of his gifts.

Saint Thomas became a great teacher, a preacher and a writer. He shared his gift of wisdom with the whole world.

Ask God to help you discover the gifts that he has given to you.

Healthy Habits in the Home

All family members have gifts and talents to share. Ask God to help you discover the gifts that he has given to you. Have a family talent show to celebrate the gifts and talents of each member of your family. Talk about how each family member's gifts show how unique and special they are.

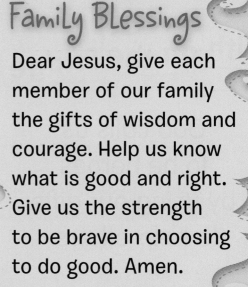

Family Blessings

Dear Jesus, give each member of our family the gifts of wisdom and courage. Help us know what is good and right. Give us the strength to be brave in choosing to do good. Amen.

Taking the Lesson Home

Share with each other something about yourself:

1. Tell something you can do well.

2. Tell about something you made by yourself.

3. Tell about something kind you did for someone.

4. Tell the nicest thing about you.

5. Tell something you did for your family.

Faith on the Fridge

God calls us
to be heroes
by using our gifts
to help others.

Family
Web Time
RCLBFamilyLife.com

There's No One Just Like You

You are one of a kind.
In all the world, there is no one
else just like you.
There will never be another you.
Isn't that great?

God loves you just as you are.
God gave you your own gifts
and talents to share.
God wants you to be yourself and
to make the most of who you are.

 Tell about one special gift that God gave you.

Gifts to Share

Each person is different.
Each person has special gifts and talents.

Jean cannot see.
She feels and hears things that
her friends never notice.

John cannot hear.
He can read lips and talk with
his hands.

Bill cannot walk.
He uses a wheelchair to go everywhere.
He can draw and sing and make
his friends laugh.

God gives everyone different gifts.
All people have gifts to share.

Catholics Believe
God gives each person
gifts to share.

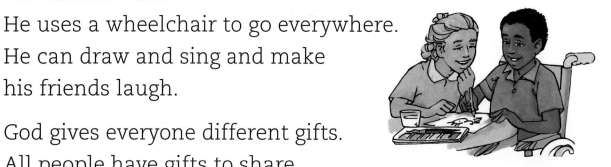

Activity

All About Me

Tell about yourself.

My name is _____ .

I can _____ .

I like to _____ .

Sharing My Special Gifts

Feel proud of who you are.

God made you special.

God gave you special gifts.

What is one special gift that you have?

How can you use that gift to help someone
in your family?

Draw yourself using your special gift
to help someone in your family.

I Can Be Brave

You Are Growing

Every day you grow and change.
It happens very slowly.
Maybe you don't feel it.
Maybe you don't think about it.
But it is happening all the time.

Your body changes.
You learn new things.
You see new things.

 How have you grown this year?

Changes

As you grow up, your body changes.
It will get bigger.
It will look and feel different.
You will have new feelings and ideas.
You will have new friends.
You will learn new things about yourself and God.
You will decide more things by yourself.

Growing up is not always easy. Making good choices is not always easy.

But God always helps you. You can be brave and happy. Life can be more exciting with each new day.

Growing in Virtue
I can be brave with God's help.

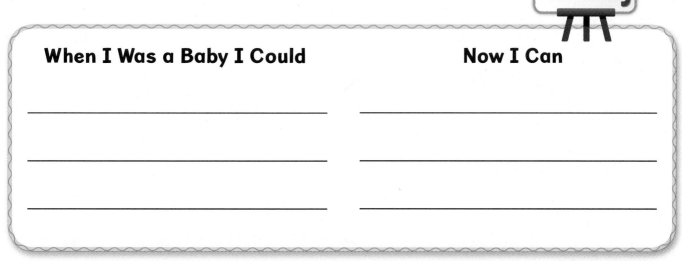

When I Was a Baby I Could	Now I Can
_____	_____
_____	_____
_____	_____

Making Good Choices

To help you make good and
brave choices, remember WALT.

Watch what others do.

Ask trusted adults and friends.

Listen to their good advice.

Think before you act.

Activity

Think about making a good choice.

Who will you WATCH?_____

Who will you ASK? _____

Who will you LISTEN TO? _____

What will you do next? _____

_____

Name _____

Summary

We have learned about God's Gift of Self.

LESSON 3: Who Are You?

- God loves me just as I am.
- God has given everyone gifts to share
- I am proud of who God made me to be.

LESSON 4: I Can Be Brave

- As I grow, my body, mind and feelings change.
- I can be brave with God's help.
- I can make good decisions.

Content Review

Complete each sentence using one word from the word bank.

act	brave	gifts	grow

1. God gives everyone unique .... and talents to share.

2. As I .... , my body changes.

3. With God's help, I can be .... in making good choices.

4. Before I make a choice, I should think before I ....

Circle the T if the statement is true.
Circle the F if the statement is false.

1. Many other people are exactly like you.   T   F
2. Sometimes it is difficult to make good choices.   T   F
3. A person who cannot see has gifts to share too.   T   F
4. You must be an adult before you can use your gifts.   T   F
5. Some people do not have any special gifts and talents.   T   F

Name _____

Thinking It Through

Read each question. Then write a short response.
Share your answers.

1. What gifts has God given me to share with others?

_____

_____

2. How does God help me to use my gifts well?

_____

_____

3. How can I tell that I am growing?

_____

_____

Working Together

Write a letter to yourself about some
of the things that you have learned.
Be sure to put your name, age and
today's date on the letter. Seal it in
an envelope and write your name on
it. Open the envelope after you have
completed the last lesson in this book.

Caring for Jesus

Jesus said that when we care for anyone, we are caring for him *(based on Matthew 25:40)*.

When you help your family, you help Jesus.

When you care for people not in your family, you care for Jesus.

Family Blessings

Dear Heavenly Father, bless all of your children. We thank you for sending your Son, Jesus. Fill our hearts with the love of the Holy Spirit. Amen.

Healthy Habits in the Home

Add to your family's list of chores ways in which your family can care for living creatures and things around your home. Take turns doing these chores by rotating the responsibilities throughout the week.

Taking the Lesson Home

Talk about these questions with your family:

1. How do we care for one another?

2. How do we remember God loves us?

3. How can we care for people not in our family?

Faith on the Fridge

Create a family prayer list and post it on the fridge. Include petitions for those in need and praise for those who have been blessed.

Family Web Time
RCLBFamilyLife.com

A Family Grows

A family can grow.
A husband and wife love
each other in a special way.
The wife becomes pregnant.
They learn a new baby is coming.
This means a baby is growing
inside the womb of the wife.
The husband and wife are now
a father and mother.
The parents make plans
for their new baby.
Their baby will need clothes,
food and a place to sleep.
Their new baby will
need lots of love.

 How do you think a wife
and her husband feel
when they have a new baby?

A Baby Is Born

It is a happy time when a baby is born.
The baby is a gift from God.
The family is blessed with new life.
The parents hold their new baby
in their arms for the first time.
The baby will grow and change.
The baby will learn to walk and talk.
The family is growing in love.
They will continue to
keep their child safe.
They will do things to
keep their child healthy.
They will teach their child about God.

Activity

Write or draw something that parents do to care for a new baby.

I Can Help

Catholic parents care for their new baby
in a special way.
They bring their baby to Mass.
They ask the Church to baptize their baby.
They teach their child about God.
They teach their child to pray.
They want their child to be happy,
healthy and holy.

Pretend you are a parent.
What will you teach your child about God?

I will_____ .

What will you teach your child about being healthy?

I will_____ .

What will you teach your child about being safe?

I will_____ .

Caring for Life

God's Wonderful Gift of Life

God created all living things.
He gave life to plants, animals and people.
God wants all of us to care for them.

When you get a gift, you take care of it.
You say, "Thank you."

You can help care for living things.
You can care for plants by watering them.
You can care for animals and pets
at home.

You can care for yourself.
You can keep yourself healthy, holy
and safe.

When you do these things, you say, "Thank
you, God, for the wonderful gift of my life."

**What living things do you help
take care of? Tell how you can
take care of them.**

The Golden Rule

Jesus taught us to care for others as we want them to care for us. This is the Golden Rule. There are different ways people care for each other. In the Church, we pray for one another. In communities, people help keep one another safe. In school, teachers and students help each other to learn.

Growing in Virtue

I can follow the Golden Rule.

Activity

Look at the pictures on the page. Talk about how the person cares. In the heart write the name of someone who cares for you.

I Can Start Now

You can care for living things.
You can start right now.
You can start at home.

Activity

Write or draw something that
each of these living things needs.

Plants	Pets	People

? What will you do to help care for them?
Ask someone at home to help you.

Name _____

Summary

We have learned about God's Gift of Life.

LESSON 5: New Life

- New life is a gift from God.
- A family grows with a new baby.
- Parents want their children to be healthy, holy and happy.

LESSON 6: Caring for Life

- God created all living things and wants us to care for them.
- The Golden Rule is to care for others as I would have them care for me.
- I can live the Golden Rule.

Content Review

Complete each sentence using one word from the word bank.

mother	gift	healthy	love

1. A baby comes from a special kind of .... between a husband and wife.

2. A baby grows inside the womb of the ....

3. A baby is a .... from God.

4. Parents keep their baby safe and ....

Circle the T if the statement is true.
Circle the F if the statement is false.

1. God created all living things.   T   F
2. You cannot help care for yourself.   T   F
3. Prayer is one way of caring for others.   T   F
4. Jesus taught us the Golden Rule.   T   F
5. The Golden Rule is to give others gold.   T   F

Name _____

Thinking It Through

Read each question. Then write a short response.
Share your answers.

1. Why is it good to care for living things?

_____

_____

2. How does the Golden Rule help you to care for others?

_____

_____

3. What can you do today to take care of a living creature?

_____

_____

Working Together

Form a small group. Each group will pretend
to be a family caring for a baby. Name the
baby and decide what the baby needs.
Tell the class the plan your family has for the baby.

God's Gift of Love

Christian Love

Jesus said that we should forgive anyone with whom we are angry. Showing love by forgiving others is not easy.

Forgiving a person who has hurt you is difficult.

But showing love is always better than getting even. And forgiving is better than staying angry.

Family Blessings

Dear Jesus, sometimes it is hard for us to tell the truth. Help us to forgive those who hurt us. Help us to show our love for one another. Amen.

Healthy Habits in the Home

At Baptism we promise to live as children of God. Create a family list of promises that help each family member live as a child of God. For example, we promise to share, forgive and tell the truth. Post the list prominently in your home.

Taking the Lesson Home

Talk about these situations with your family:

1. You promise to wake up for school on time. How can you keep that promise?

2. You promise to go to a friend's party. How can you keep that promise?

3. You promise to fix a meal by yourself. How can you keep that promise?

4. You promise to finish all your homework. How can you keep that promise?

Faith on the Fridge

My God, I love you
above all things. I love you
with my whole heart and soul.
I love my neighbor as myself
for the love of you.
I forgive all who have hurt me,
and I ask forgiveness of all
whom I have hurt. Amen.

Family Web Time
RCLBFamilyLife.com

Signs of Love

Showing Our Love

You cannot see love.
You cannot hear love, or smell it,
or taste it or touch it.
So how can you show love?
You can do things that are signs of love.
You show love with kind words.
You show love with fair actions.
Families find ways to show their love
for each other and for God.

 What can you do to show love to your family?

Making Things Better

Catholics Believe

Sacraments are signs of love between God and us.

Have you ever had a time when it was not easy to show love? Everyone has times like that. What can you do?

You can think about what went wrong. You can do something to make it better. You can say, "I'm sorry" or "I forgive you." Then you can try to do better next time.

The Church helps us make things better in a very special way. We celebrate the Sacrament of Penance and Reconciliation. God gives us his forgiveness. God gives us his help, or grace, to make things better.

Activity

Write the names of those people who can help you when things go wrong.

_____

_____

_____

_____

_____

_____

What Can We Do?

Families show love in many ways.
But sometimes they might forget.
They might do or say things
that do not show love.
They might get mad and yell at each other.
They might hurt each other.
When this happens, what can family
members do to make things better?

Activity

Each letter has a special color.
Put each letter in the right box.
Discover a way to show love.

A M E K   E C A P E

Promises

Wedding Vows

Have you ever gone to a wedding or seen one on television? What did you see and hear? What is the most important part of the wedding?

 Tell what is happening in the picture.

The most important part of the wedding is when the bride and groom make their promises to each other. They promise to be truthful to each other. They promise to care for one another no matter how difficult. They promise to keep their promises forever. They promise to love each other forever. They give each other a ring as a sign of their love. They ask God to help them keep their promises.

The New Family

When a man and a woman marry,
they include God in their marriage.
They start a new life together.
They become a new family.
They share, pray and plan together.
They learn new things about each
other as their love grows.
They remember the promises they
made on their wedding day.
Sometimes they might not agree.
So they talk things over.
They try to understand
each other better.
They show forgiving love.

Growing in Virtue

I can make a promise to my
parents as a sign of my
love for them.

When a man and a woman
marry, they exchange rings
as a sign of their love.

Color the word "LOVE"
inside the rings.

I Keep My Promises

What is a promise?

A promise puts love in words.

You say something good that you want to do.

Then you do your best to keep your promise.

If you forget to keep your promise, you do
your best to try again.

You can ask God to help
you keep your promise.

Here is a list of family promises.
Tell how you can help keep these promises.
Choose one of these promises.
Write one way you will keep it.

We promise to share.

We promise to be fair.

We promise to help one another.

We promise to tell the truth.

I promise to _____.

I will_____.

Name_____

Summary

We have learned about God's Gift of Love.

LESSON 7: Signs of Love

- I can show love with words and actions.
- Sacraments are signs of love between God and us.
- I can say and do things to make things better.

LESSON 8: Promises

- The promises a husband and wife make are the most important part of the wedding.
- Family members need to work at understanding each other.
- I can make a promise to my family as a sign of my love.

Content Review

Complete each sentence using one word from the word bank.

actions	God	love	ring

1. Sacraments are signs of .... between God and us.

2. We show love through our words and ....

3. .... helps us keep our promises.

4. The wedding .... is a sign of the love between a husband and wife.

Circle the T if the statement is true.
Circle the F if the statement is false.

1. The party is the most important part of a wedding.   T   F

2. When a man and a woman marry, they become a new family. T   F

3. A husband and wife promise to care for each other forever.   T   F

4. Sometimes it is not easy to show love.   T   F

Name_____

Thinking It Through

Read each question. Then write a short response.
Share your answers.

1. Why should you think carefully before you make a promise?

   _____

   _____

2. What can you do when you do not keep a promise?

   _____

   _____

3. How can you show love to your family?

   _____

   _____

Working Together

Tell about a time when it was hard to say,
"I'm sorry." Talk about the ways you can
show that you are sorry.

God's Gift of Community

Hope in the Lord

God is with our family at all times.
He is with us in happy times
and sad times.
Sometimes it may seem
that God is far away.
God is never far away.
The Prophet Isaiah said, "Trust
in the Lord and he will give
you strength" (based on Isaiah 26:4).
Remember that God is always
near us and always loves us.

Family Blessings

Dear God, we know
that you are here
with us today.
Whatever happens
to us, we trust in
you. You give us
strength and keep
us safe. Amen.

Healthy Habits in the Home

When you are watching shows,
movies or videos together, look
for people who are treating
one another as good friends.
Discuss why these characters
are good role models on how
to be a good friend.

Taking the Lesson Home

Talk about these questions with your family:

1. What do you like best to do with your family?

2. What do you like best to do with a friend?

3. What do you like best to do with your parish family?

Faith on the Fridge

Jesus said,
"I am with you always."

(Matthew 28:20)

Family Web Time
RCLBFamilyLife.com

Family Connections

Let's Celebrate

All families have happy times.
They celebrate together as a family.
Each family celebrates
in their own unique way.
Family celebrations say,
"We care about one another."
How does your family celebrate
these special events?

    Easter
    Christmas
    Birthdays
    Weddings

 What is your favorite family celebration?

Happy Times, Sad Times

Catholics Believe

God is with families during their happy times and their sad times.

All families have happy times.
All families have sad times, too.
Maybe someone is sick or has died.
Maybe parents are separated
or divorced.
Families try to help each other
during happy and sad times.
Each family helps in its own way.
Helping each other says, "We care
about one another."

Activity

Read each question.
Write your answer on the line.

Who helps you in sad times?

_____

Who do you share your happy times with?

_____

We Rejoice and Help

Read the stories below.
If it is a time to rejoice together,
print an **R** in the circle.
If it is a time to help one another,
print an **H** in the circle.

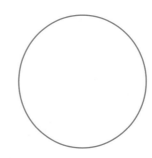

A grandfather has died.
We visit Grandmother.

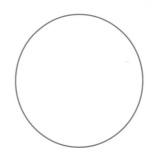

An aunt and uncle have a new baby.
We are invited to the Baptism.

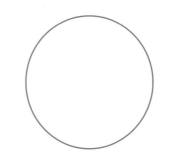

There was a fire at a cousin's house.
We bring food and other things they need.

More Connections

Your Parish Family

You belong to your family.
You belong to other groups too.
People in these groups
care for one another.
They show love for one another.
This makes them like families.

You are part of a school family.
You are part of a neighborhood family.
You are part of a parish family.

Your parish family celebrates God's love.
Your parish family shares God's love
with you and with your family.
Your parish shares God's love with
the People of God, the Church,
all over the world.

Activity

Tell how you show that you are part of your family.

_____

Tell how you show that you are part of your parish family.

_____

Being a Friend

You are important to
all of your families.
As you grow, you learn how
to share and help others.
You learn to be friends.

Everyone needs friends.
Everyone likes to have friends.
Your friends can be young, old
and every age in-between.

Friends work and play together.
They learn from each other.
Friends are fair to each other.
Friends tell the truth to each other.
Friends may disagree,
but they can make up.
Friends make peace with each other.

Activity

Growing in Virtue
I can be fair to my friends.

Draw pictures of two ways to show that you are someone's friend.

What Have You Learned?

You belong to many groups that are like families. Tell something you have learned from each of these families.

From my school family, I have learned

_____ .

From my neighborhood family, I have learned

_____ .

From my parish family, I have learned

_____ .

From my family at home, I have learned

_____ .

From my friends, I have learned

_____

_____ .

Name_____

Summary

We have learned about God's Gift of Community.

LESSON 9: Family Connections

- Families celebrate happy times together.
- Families support and help each other in sad times.
- God is with us in happy and sad times.

LESSON 10: More Connections

- I belong to groups that are like families.
- God wants us to treat one another as friends.
- I can be a friend to others.

Content Review

Circle the best word to complete each sentence.

1. Neighborhoods, school and parishes are like (families, parties).

2. You are an (invisible, important) member in all of your families.

3. Everybody needs (the Internet, friends).

4. You (can, cannot) be friends with an older person.

5. You can (take, learn) things from friends.

6. Friends should (make peace, stay angry) when they disagree.

7. During the year, families (celebrate, forget) special events.

8. God is (always, never) with us during sad times.

9. Easter is an event to be (happy, sad).

10. Friends want (good, bad) things for one another.

Name_____

Thinking It Through

Read each question. Then write a short response.
Share your answers.

1. Why is it important for a family to celebrate?

_____

_____

2. How could you help if a family member got very sick?

_____

_____

3. How does your parish family help others in need?

_____

_____

Working Together

Help a class friend think of a good way
to send a message of love to their parish
family. Then send that message to the
pastor of the parish.

Name _____

Content Review

Complete each sentence by using one word from the word bank

ring	gift	friends	act	family

1. God loves every ....

2. Before I make a choice, I should think before I ....

3. A baby is a .... from God.

4. The wedding .... is a sign of the love between a husband and wife.

5. God wants us to treat one another as ....

Circle the T if the statement is true.
Circle the F if the statement is false.

1. Jesus gave us rules to keep families happy and safe.   T   F

2. Some people do not have any special gifts or talents   T   F

3. Prayer is one way of caring for others.   T   F

4. When a man and a woman marry,
   they become a new family.   T   F

5. Friends want bad things for one another.   T   F

Name _____

Thinking It Through

Read each question. Then write a short response.
Share your answers.

1. What can I do if I think a rule is not good?

_____

2. How does God help me to use my gifts well?

_____

3. Why is it good to have rules?

_____

4. What happens when I do not keep a promise?

_____

5. Why is it important for a family to celebrate?

_____

Working Together

In groups write a list of petitions
for the whole class to offer in prayer
as a way to celebrate the end of this
year's learning.

Name _____

Summary

We have learned about Family Life this year.

God's Gift of Family

- God loves every kind of family.
- Good rules keep us healthy, holy and safe.
- I can obey good rules.

God's Gift of Self

- God has given everyone gifts to share.
- I am proud of who God made me to be.
- I can be brave and make good choices with God's help.

God's Gift of Life

- New life is a gift from God.
- God created all living things and wants us to care for them.
- I can live the Golden Rule.

God's Gift of Love

- Sacraments are signs of love between God and us.
- Families need to work at understanding each other.
- I can make a promise to my family as a sign of my love.

God's Gift of Community

- God is with us in happy and sad times.
- Families support and help each other.
- I can be a friend to others.

Recognition of Achievement

The faith community of

_____

proudly announces

_____

and family have completed the second level of
RCL Benziger Family Life.

This young person has discovered:
God's gift of family
God's gift of self
God's gift of life
God's gift of love
God's gift of community

May every day provide you and your family new adventures
in following Jesus and in living faithful Christian lives.

_____

(Signed)